WELCOME
ULTRA HEROES
BLACK ICE
EDITION

Your journey to becoming a comic artist has begun. You will absolutely enjoy this easy 4-step instruction book and be well on your way to becoming a drawing genius. So grab your paper and pencil and let's get started!!!

Things you will need:

Pencil

Eraser

Paper

Black ink pen

Things you may want to use:

Scrap paper

Pencil crayons

Markers

Remember to press lightly when drawing, to make your extra lines easier to erase when you are finished.

STEP I: LAYOUT OF YOUR CHARACTERS

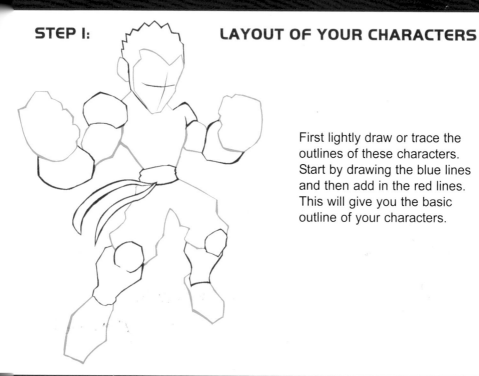

First lightly draw or trace the outlines of these characters. Start by drawing the blue lines and then add in the red lines. This will give you the basic outline of your characters.

1

STEP 2:   DEFINING YOUR CHARACTERS

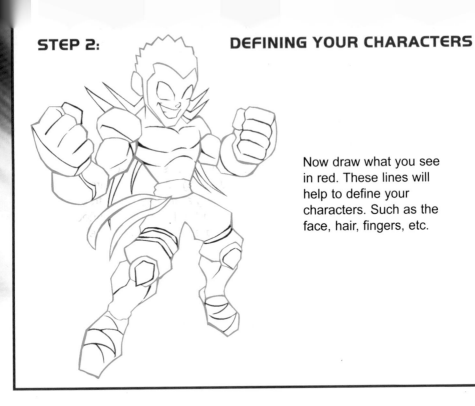

Now draw what you see in red. These lines will help to define your characters. Such as the face, hair, fingers, etc.

STEP 3:   DETAILING YOUR CHARACTERS

Now that you have finished the bigger details for your characters, you are going to add in the smaller details.

Draw what you see here in red.

STEP 4: INKING YOUR CHARACTERS

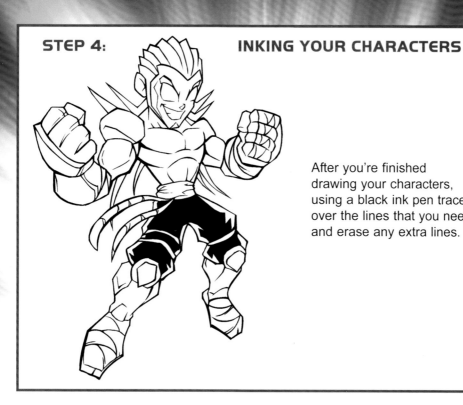

After you're finished drawing your characters, using a black ink pen trace over the lines that you need, and erase any extra lines.

COLORING YOUR CHARACTERS

When coloring your characters start by using the lightest color as your base, and then add darker colors for shading. You can use pencil crayons or markers to color your characters.

FREEZE

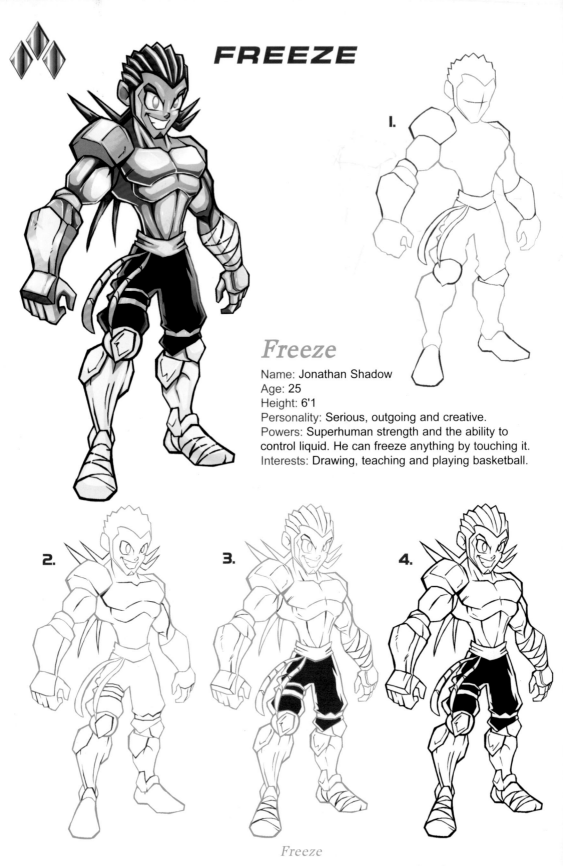

I.

Freeze

Name: Jonathan Shadow
Age: 25
Height: 6'1
Personality: Serious, outgoing and creative.
Powers: Superhuman strength and the ability to control liquid. He can freeze anything by touching it.
Interests: Drawing, teaching and playing basketball.

2.

3.

4.

Freeze

is the oldest of the Shadow brother's and the leader of the Blac Ice family, he put the team together with the help of his mentor Kirk Peterson and they are helping to conquer the quest for world peace. In his spare time he teaches children how to draw and has created his own line of children's drawing books.

4

STERLING

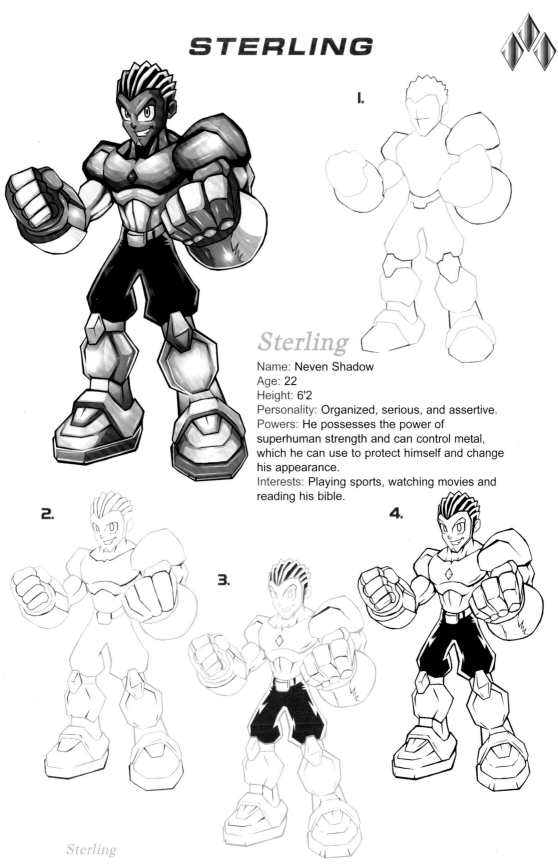

I.

Sterling

Name: Neven Shadow
Age: 22
Height: 6'2
Personality: Organized, serious, and assertive.
Powers: He possesses the power of superhuman strength and can control metal, which he can use to protect himself and change his appearance.
Interests: Playing sports, watching movies and reading his bible.

2.

3.

4.

Sterling

is the Shadow brother who keeps everyone on the team focused and in order. When he is not training he likes to go to church and he enjoys playing basketball with Freeze and Mad Puncher.

CYLONG

1.

Cylong

Name: Gemini Shadow
Age:18 Height: 6'4
Personality: Fun, outgoing and caring.
Powers: He has the ability to control fire and shoot fire from his eyes. He also possesses superhuman speed.
Interests: Computers, playing video games and martial arts.

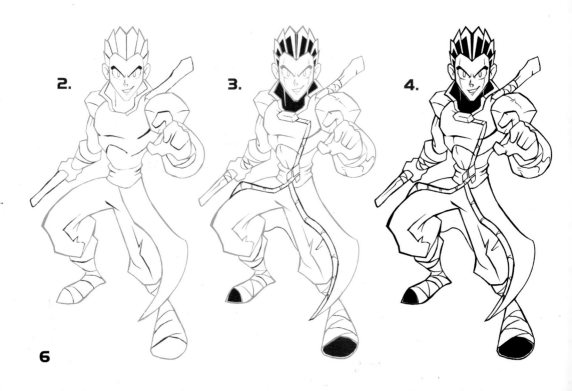

2.

3.

4.

CYLONG

1.

2.

3.

4.

Cylong

is the youngest of The Shadow Brother's, he loves that he has his powers and can help the family with their quest for world peace. Although sometimes he can be a little carefree and likes to show off a bit too much, he is still an important member of the team. He is currently helping Little K start her singing career by producing her first album.

Time Wave

Name: Helen Wright
Age: 21
Height: 5'4
Personality: Quiet, shy and fun-loving.
Powers: She has the ability to travel through time and often uses her powers to show her opponents, what their future will hold if they do the wrong thing.
Interests: Traveling, writing, and singing.

3.

2.

4.

Time Wave

has unique time traveling powers and is able to show her opponents what their future would hold if they do the wrong thing. Although she is a bit quiet, and often disappears to go shopping for the latest deals with Little K, she is always around when the team needs her.

LITTLE K

Little K

Name: Kayla Charles
Age: 19
Height: 5'6
Personality: Outgoing, popular and independent.
Powers: Telekinesis, the ability to move objects with her mind as well as superhuman strength.
Interests: Singing, acting and dancing.

I.

2.

3.

4.

Little K

is one of the world's most beloved superheroes and now one of The Blac Ice Families most valued team members. Freeze met with her personally and asked her to join the team and she couldn't have been happier, she was on her own mission for world peace but enjoys working with others more then working alone.

1.

2.

3.

4.

Lite Wing

Name: Emma Rose
Age: 20
Height: 5'2
Personality: Quiet, friendly, and cheerful.
Powers: She has the ability to fly extremely fast.
Interests: Ballet dancing, ice skating, and baking.

Lite Wing

agreed to join the Blac Ice team a few years ago after discovering her abilities, she is still learning how to fully use her powers but she has helped the Blac Ice Family on a few of their missions thus far.

BLUE STREAK

Blue Streak

Name: Joshua Clark
Age: 15
Height: 5'11
Personality: Quiet, serious and dependable.
Powers: He has the ability to run and move extremely fast and also has superhuman reflexes.
Interests: Science, studying and playing hockey.

Blue Streak

is one of the youngest members of the Blac Ice Family but he is extremely smart, he is very interested in becoming a scientist and has been assisting Reggie Sparks while he is in high school and before he goes to college.

I.

2.

3.

4.

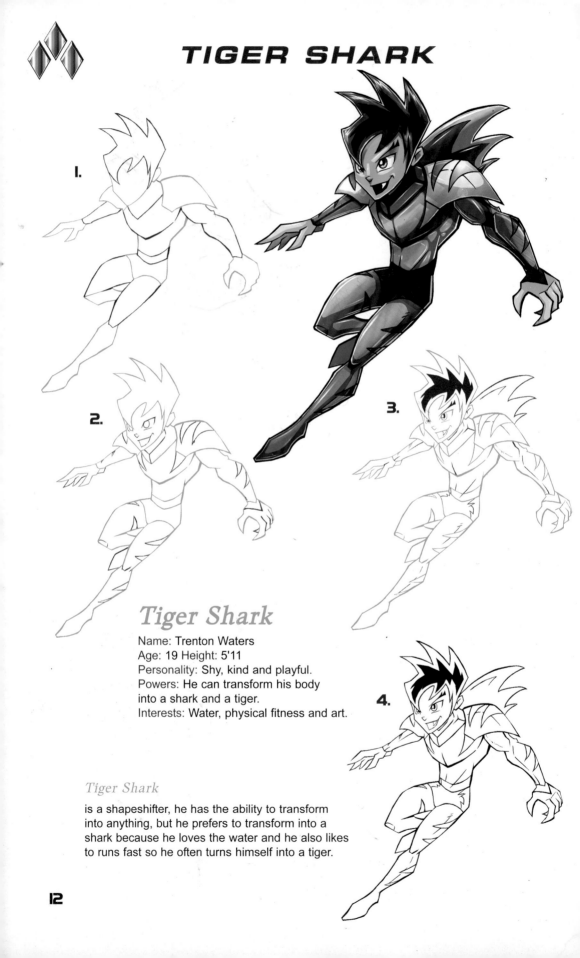

TIGER SHARK

1.

2.

3.

4.

Tiger Shark

Name: Trenton Waters
Age: 19 Height: 5'11
Personality: Shy, kind and playful.
Powers: He can transform his body
into a shark and a tiger.
Interests: Water, physical fitness and art.

Tiger Shark

is a shapeshifter, he has the ability to transform
into anything, but he prefers to transform into a
shark because he loves the water and he also likes
to runs fast so he often turns himself into a tiger.

1.

2.

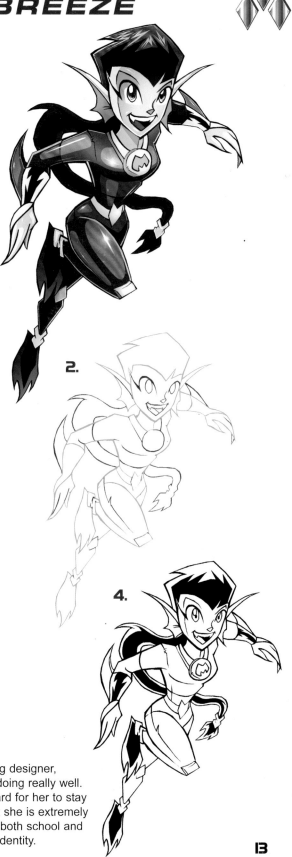

3.

4.

Sea Breeze

Name: Eternity Stone
Age: 20 Height: 5'7
Personality: Creative, sensitive and kind.´
Powers: She has the ability to turn into a mermaid and communicate with all other sea creatures.
Interests: Designing clothes, writing stories and shopping with friends.

Sea Breeze

is in school to become a clothing designer, she really loves fashion and is doing really well. Although sometimes it's a bit hard for her to stay focused when on a mission, but she is extremely smart and manages to balance both school and work, while keeping her secret identity.

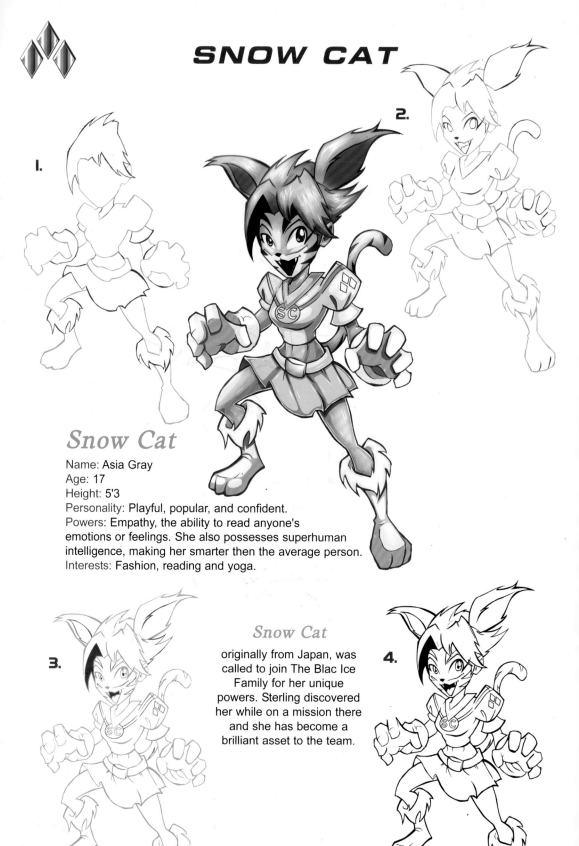

Snow Cat

Name: Asia Gray
Age: 17
Height: 5'3
Personality: Playful, popular, and confident.
Powers: Empathy, the ability to read anyone's emotions or feelings. She also possesses superhuman intelligence, making her smarter then the average person.
Interests: Fashion, reading and yoga.

Snow Cat

originally from Japan, was called to join The Blac Ice Family for her unique powers. Sterling discovered her while on a mission there and she has become a brilliant asset to the team.

1.
2.
3.
4.

MAD PUNCHER

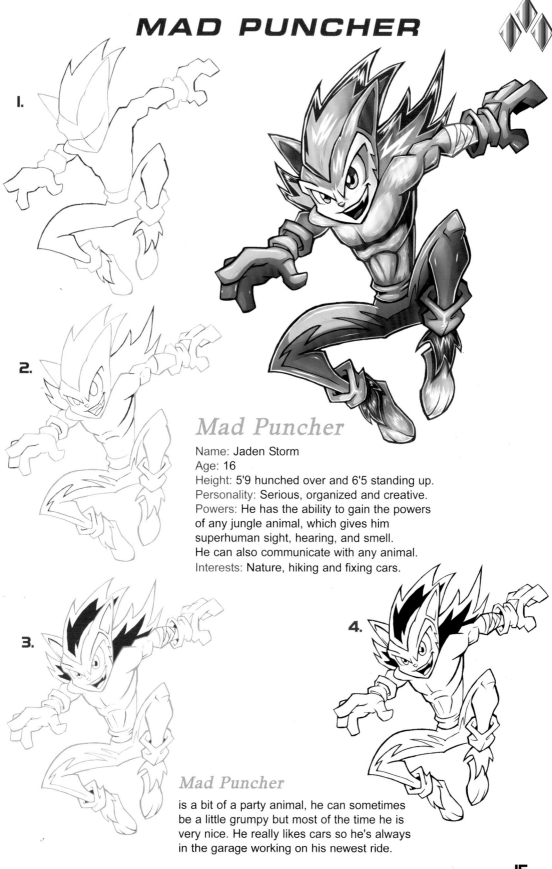

1.

2.

Mad Puncher

Name: Jaden Storm
Age: 16
Height: 5'9 hunched over and 6'5 standing up.
Personality: Serious, organized and creative.
Powers: He has the ability to gain the powers
of any jungle animal, which gives him
superhuman sight, hearing, and smell.
He can also communicate with any animal.
Interests: Nature, hiking and fixing cars.

3.

4.

Mad Puncher

is a bit of a party animal, he can sometimes
be a little grumpy but most of the time he is
very nice. He really likes cars so he's always
in the garage working on his newest ride.

I.

Sand Storm

Name: Tyler McGinnis
Age: 25 Height: 6'
Personality: Smart, independent and friendly.
Powers: He has superhuman intelligence.
Interests: Reading, surfing and computers.

2.

3.

4.

Sand Storm

is a super genius, when he was 17 years old he developed a suit that is made of fibres that are as strong as steel, when he wears the suit it gives him his superpowers and also protects him.

ICE

Ice

Name: Reggie Sparks
Age: 31
Height: 6'2
Personality: Fun, outgoing, and noble.
Powers: He has the ability to fly, as well as superhuman speed and super strength.
Interests: Science, animals and traveling.

I.

2.

3.

4.

Ice

is a scientist, while he was in the arctic studying animals he found what turned out to be a meteor, which gave him his superpowers. He felt it was his duty to help mankind, so he joined The Blac Ice Team.

MA KAYLA

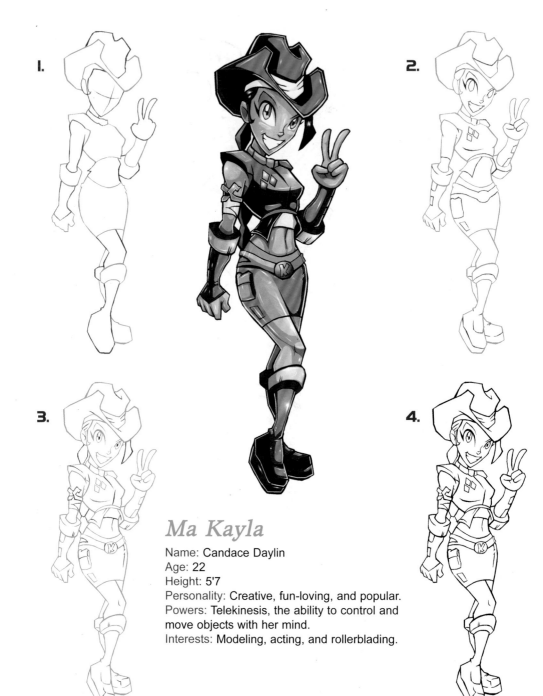

1.

2.

3.

4.

Ma Kayla

Name: Candace Daylin
Age: 22
Height: 5'7
Personality: Creative, fun-loving, and popular.
Powers: Telekinesis, the ability to control and move objects with her mind.
Interests: Modeling, acting, and rollerblading.

Ma Kayla

is a well known model and actress, when she is not modeling or acting she is helping out The Blac Ice Family, she is very intelligent and has been able to figure out how to use her powers to their full potential.

SPARKLE

1.

2.

3.

4.

Sparkle

Name: Trinity Springs
Age: 200 years old Height: 3'5
Personality: Fun, resourceful and independent.
Powers: She possesses magical powers, the
ability to use magical forces to varying degrees
and she also never ages.
Interests: Gardening, dancing, and singing.

Sparkle

is a 200 year old fairy, she is from another dimension called "Wonderland" although
she is extremely wise she sometimes uses her magical powers to play tricks on the
other team members, mostly Mad Puncher and Cylong.

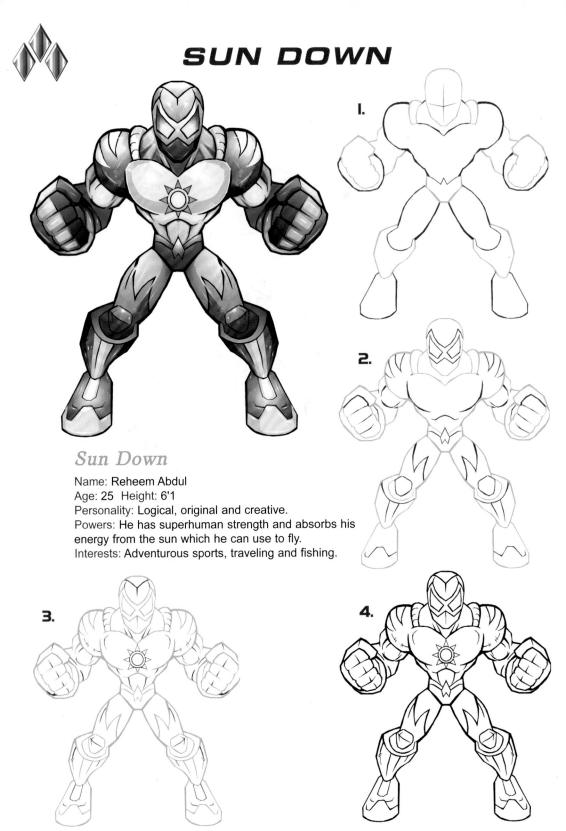

SUN DOWN

1.

2.

Sun Down

Name: Reheem Abdul
Age: 25 Height: 6'1
Personality: Logical, original and creative.
Powers: He has superhuman strength and absorbs his energy from the sun which he can use to fly.
Interests: Adventurous sports, traveling and fishing.

3.

4.

Sun Down

is one of the strongest members of the team he uses his strength to help train the rest of the team. When he's not out trying to save the world you can often find him at the beach with Sand Storm and Sea Breeze soaking up the sun.

JAM ROCK

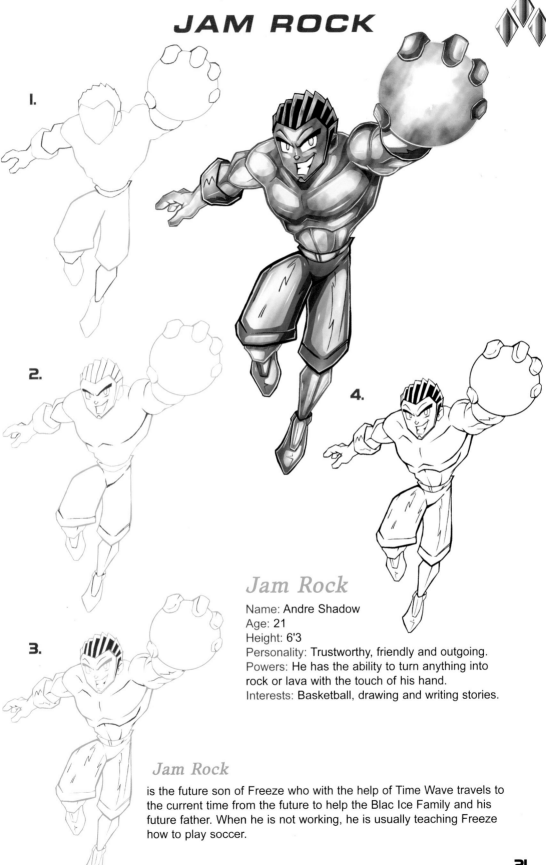

I.

2.

3.

4.

Jam Rock

Name: Andre Shadow
Age: 21
Height: 6'3
Personality: Trustworthy, friendly and outgoing.
Powers: He has the ability to turn anything into rock or lava with the touch of his hand.
Interests: Basketball, drawing and writing stories.

Jam Rock

is the future son of Freeze who with the help of Time Wave travels to the current time from the future to help the Blac Ice Family and his future father. When he is not working, he is usually teaching Freeze how to play soccer.

FREEZE

Jonathan Shadow
Powers: Ice and liquid

ABILITIES 1 2 3 4 5 6 7 8
INTELLIGENCE
STRENGTH
SPEED
DURABILITY
POWER LEVEL

STERLING

Neven Shadow
Powers: Controls Metal

ABILITIES 1 2 3 4 5 6 7 8
INTELLIGENCE
STRENGTH
SPEED
DURABILITY
POWER LEVEL

CYLONG

Gemini Shadow
Powers: Controls Fire

ABILITIES 1 2 3 4 5 6 7 8
INTELLIGENCE
STRENGTH
SPEED
DURABILITY
POWER LEVEL

TIME WAVE

Helen Wright
Powers: Time Travel

ABILITIES 1 2 3 4 5 6 7 8
INTELLIGENCE
STRENGTH
SPEED
DURABILITY
POWER LEVEL

LITTLE K

Kayla Charles
Powers: Telekinesis

ABILITIES 1 2 3 4 5 6 7 8
INTELLIGENCE
STRENGTH
SPEED
DURABILITY
POWER LEVEL

LITE WING

Emma Rose
Powers: Flight

ABILITIES 1 2 3 4 5 6 7 8
INTELLIGENCE
STRENGTH
SPEED
DURABILITY
POWER LEVEL

BLUE STREAK

Joshua Clark
Powers: Super Speed

ABILITIES 1 2 3 4 5 6 7 8
INTELLIGENCE
STRENGTH
SPEED
DURABILITY
POWER LEVEL

TIGER SHARK

Trenton Waters
Powers: Shapeshifter

ABILITIES 1 2 3 4 5 6 7 8
INTELLIGENCE
STRENGTH
SPEED
DURABILITY
POWER LEVEL

SEA BREEZE

Eternity Stone
Powers: Mermaid

ABILITIES 1 2 3 4 5 6 7 8
INTELLIGENCE
STRENGTH
SPEED
DURABILITY
POWER LEVEL

THE BLAC ICE FAMILY

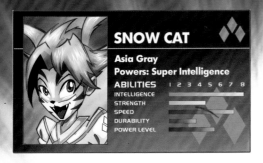

SNOW CAT

Asia Gray
Powers: Super Intelligence
ABILITIES 1 2 3 4 5 6 7 8
INTELLIGENCE
STRENGTH
SPEED
DURABILITY
POWER LEVEL

MAD PUNCHER

Jaden Storm
Powers: Jungle Animals
ABILITIES 1 2 3 4 5 6 7 8
INTELLIGENCE
STRENGTH
SPEED
DURABILITY
POWER LEVEL

SAND STORM

Tyler McGinnis
Powers: Super Genius
ABILITIES 1 2 3 4 5 6 7 8
INTELLIGENCE
STRENGTH
SPEED
DURABILITY
POWER LEVEL

ICE

Reggie Sparks
Powers: Super Strength
ABILITIES 1 2 3 4 5 6 7 8
INTELLIGENCE
STRENGTH
SPEED
DURABILITY
POWER LEVEL

MA KAYLA

Candace Daylin
Powers: Mind Control
ABILITIES 1 2 3 4 5 6 7 8
INTELLIGENCE
STRENGTH
SPEED
DURABILITY
POWER LEVEL

SPARKLE

Trinity Springs
Powers: Magic
ABILITIES 1 2 3 4 5 6 7 8
INTELLIGENCE
STRENGTH
SPEED
DURABILITY
POWER LEVEL

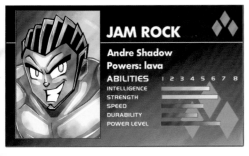

JAM ROCK

Andre Shadow
Powers: lava
ABILITIES 1 2 3 4 5 6 7 8
INTELLIGENCE
STRENGTH
SPEED
DURABILITY
POWER LEVEL

Sun Down

Reheem Abdul
Powers: Super Strength
ABILITIES 1 2 3 4 5 6 7 8
INTELLIGENCE
STRENGTH
SPEED
DURABILITY
POWER LEVEL

*Now that you've had a chance to meet the members of
The Blac Ice Family, its time to create your own Ultra Heroes!
Remember to give your character's their own personalities,
interests, powers and Ultra Hero names.*

Have fun and enjoy your drawings!

Practice page

Interested in creating your own comic book? Try our other drawing book series "Create Your Own Comic Book 1" and "Create Your Own Comic Book 2: Heroes and Villains".

Practice by drawing or tracing the figures on this page. In time you will notice you have developed your very own drawing style!

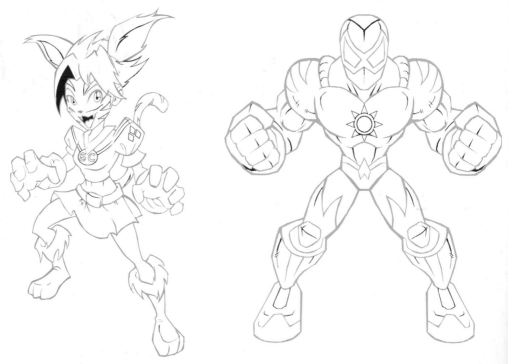

Tip: Remember, practicing often will help to improve your drawing skills.